بسم الله الرحمن الرحيم

In the name of God, the All-Beneficent, the Ever-Merciful

TAJWĪD

A GUIDE TO QUR'ANIC RECITATION

Shaykh Rizwan Arastu

ISBN 978-0-9847050-0-9

Published by Imam Mahdi Association of Marjaeya
835 Mason St.
Dearborn, MI 48124
Tel: 313-562-IMAM (4626)
www.imam-us.org

Layout and Cover Design by Islamic Publishing House (www.iph.ca)

Printed in Canada

Contents

Transliteration

Arabic has been transliterated according to the following key:

ء	a, u, or i (initial form)	ط	ṭ
ء	ʾ (medial or final form)	ظ	ẓ
ب	b	ع	ʿ
ت	t	غ	gh
ث	th	ف	f
ج	j	ق	q
ح	ḥ	ك	k
خ	kh	ل	l
د	d	م	m
ذ	dh	ن	n
ر	r	ه	h
ز	z	و	w (as a consonant)
س	s	ي	y (as a consonant)
ش	sh	ة	ah (without *iḍāfah*)
ص	ṣ	ة	at (with *iḍāfah*)
ض	ḍ	ٱل	al-

Foreword

By Sayyid Muhammad Rizvi

I.M.A.M. is striving to serve the Muslim community in North America in different ways. One plan is to publish outstanding works of literature that meaningfully contribute to Islam's rich academic and spiritual heritage.

It is our belief that *Tajwīd: A Guide to Qurʾānic Recitation* contributes to the attainment of this goal and will become a means for Muslims to recite the Qurʾān more faithfully and beautifully.

We commend Shaykh Rizwan Arastu for his efforts in revamping a centuries-old pedagogy for teaching Qurʾānic recitation. He has covered all the topics of *tajwīd* in an innovative way that is at once engaging for the modern reader and faithful to the classical works in the field.

May the Almighty bless the book's author and its readers, and grant us all the wisdom and the will to follow the teachings of the Qur'ān and the Prophet's example as personified in the Twelve Imāms from his progeny.

March 2, 2011

Sayyid Muhammad Rizvi

Introduction

Since the Qurʾān's revelation to the Prophet Muḥammad—may God shower him and his family with mercy—Muslims have been engaged in studying every aspect of this book. Insofar as the Qurʾān is a divine scripture, the vast majority of these efforts have been expended to uncover the meaning of its words and the guidance latent within them. In particular, Arabic grammar was born of an effort to codify and encapsulate the language of the Arabs in its pristine form. Lexicographers scoured the deserts of Arabia to record word usage by nomads whose language had not yet been compromised by foreign elements. Traditionists recorded and transmitted sayings from the Prophet, the imams, and their companions, which expounded difficult verses and explained correct application of verses to real situations.

While meaning and guidance have always been the most important elements of the Qurʾān, certain aesthetic elements have also received considerable attention, and these have provided the impetus for the development of much of Islamic art. In particular, I speak of Arabic calligraphy and the art of reciting the Qur'ān, *tajwīd*. It is the latter that is the topic of this book.

Tajwīd is an Arabic term that means "beautification." It refers to the science and art of reciting the Qur'ān correctly and beautifully. From the early days of Islam, it became important to codify the sounds of letters and conventions followed by native Arabs so that non-Arabs would be able to correctly and accurately recite the Qur'ān, in many cases, despite their utter ignorance of the meaning of the words. After all, it is the duty of every Muslim, regardless of his native language, to correctly recite two short chapters of the Qur'ān in Arabic five times a day in his prayers. It is for this reason that hundreds of books have been composed about *tajwīd*. These books describe, in exquisite detail, precisely how to pronounce each and every letter: its point of articulation, its attributes, how it interacts with adjoining letters, when it must be stretched or blended, made thick or thin, and how and when one must pause or stop. No aspect of recitation was left to be corrupted by foreign elements.

The science of *tajwīd*, as an institution, has withstood the test of time. Islam has now spread to every corner of the earth, and the faithful are still able to recite the Qur'ān, in many cases just as a native Arab of the 6th Century CE would have done. Even in places where "Arabic" is spoken, while the vernacular language has evolved and become a language as distant from the Qur'ān as any non-Arab language, Qur'anic Arabic has been preserved as if in a time capsule, guarded from the assault of time and tongue.

This book is an attempt to communicate the most important rules of *tajwīd* to an English-speaking audience with clarity and without the use of more Arabic terminology than absolutely necessary. This book does not aim to teach you how to read Arabic. Rather, it assumes a basic level of proficiency in Arabic reading. I have tried to give you enough information so that you can read and understand it on your own. However, as with most skills, especially linguistic ones, you will be best served by studying it with a proficient, if not qualified, teacher.

I would like to thank the Imam Mahdi Association of Marjaeya (I.M.A.M.) for commissioning this much needed book. I would also like to thank Professor Yasir Ibrahim, Associate Professor of Religion at Montclair State University, with whom I had the brief pleasure of spending one semester at Princeton as he began his doctoral studies and I completed my bachelor's degree. His detailed and thorough review of my manuscript shed light on its shortcomings and made for a more complete and beneficial book.

Points of Articulation

(makhārij al-ḥurūf)

One of the first challenges you will face when learning to recite the Qur'ān is how to pronounce Arabic letters, many of which have no parallel in English. As with any foreign language, you must make your strongest effort to adopt its new sounds and pronounce them as a native speaker would. However, there is an added urgency to this effort in Arabic, since correct pronunciation of at least a portion of the Qur'ān is a prerequisite of the daily prayers.[1]

To fully explain how to pronounce each letter, we must spend some time analyzing each one's point of articulation (*makhraj*). A letter's point of articulation comprises the parts of the mouth used to pronounce it and the position and movement of those

[1] al-Sīstānī, ʿAlī. *Minhāj al-ṣāliḥīn.* vol.1 p.207, issue 606.

parts as the letter is sounded. To make this task easier, I am going to divide the 28 letters of the Arabic alphabet into ten groups, each of which contains letters sharing a common point of articulation.

Group I - The Long Vowels:

ي	و	ا

The three long vowels: *alif, wāw,* and *yā',* are simply extensions of the three short vowels: *fatḥah, ḍammah,* and *kasrah.* Accordingly, there is no difference between the sound of each short vowel and the long vowel associated with it except of course its length. This is important to mention, as some languages (Persian and Urdu, for instance) have a tendency to pronounce the short vowels and long vowels differently.

All six vowel sounds are articulated through the central cavity of the mouth. It is worth noting that the Arabic vowels, unlike the English vowels, never come at the beginning of a syllable. For this reason, it is impossible to pronounce them without tacking them on to a consonant. This fact may come as a surprise, since most Arabic primers for children begin by incorrectly teaching them "*alif* for *arnab.*" They should instead teach them, "*hamzah* for *arnab.*"

With all this in mind, I present to you examples of the short and long vowels tacked on to the consonant *hamzah*.

Short Vowels		**Long Vowels**	
أَ	ă like the *a* in attempt	ءَا	ă like the *a* in apple
أُ	ü like the *ou* in toupee	أُو	ü like the *u* in drupe
إِ	ē like the *y* in easy	إِي	ē like the *ea* in easy and beat

It is important to note that *alif* is not always pronounced with a thin sound, like the *a* in apple, as I have indicated in the table above. Sometimes it must be pronounced with a thick sound like the *aw* in "raw" and "thaw" as I shall indicate later in this chapter. However, since it is predominantly pronounced with a thin sound, I have taken the liberty of saying it is like the *a* in apple. It is noteworthy that people with an Iraqi, Persian, or Urdu background have a tendency to mispronounce the *alif* as a thick letter always. This should be avoided.

It is also important to note that people with a Turkish background have a tendency to pronounce the long vowel *wāw* similar to the German umlaut by moving the lips forward more than what is required in its Arabic pronunciation. This should also be avoided.

Group II – The Labial Consonants:

ف	و	م	ب

As their name suggests, these consonants are all pronounced from the lips. Fortunately, they are articulated exactly like the letters *b, m, w,* and *f* in English, so we need not say much about them.

Some people find it difficult to pronounce the و. Because this letter is pronounced in Urdu and Persian with a distinct flavor of a *v*, people with those backgrounds tend to mispronounce it in Arabic. To pronounce the و correctly, you should pucker your lips as if to whistle. Then draw your lips back slightly as you say the letter. Your bottom lip should never touch your top incisors, or the sound will turn to the notorious Persian and Urdu *vāv*, instead of *wāw*.

You will notice that this is the second time I have mentioned و in these lists. When و has a *sukūn* it acts like a long vowel and belongs in Group I. When it has a short vowel on it, it is a consonant and belongs here in Group II.

Group III –The Throat Consonants:

خ	غ	ح	ع	ه	ء

These six consonants are pronounced from the throat. Let us divide them into three pairs, each of which has its own point of articulation within the throat: the lower throat, the middle throat, and the upper throat. It will behoove you to memorize these six letters in the same order in which I have presented them (beginning with ء), since this is the order of their articulation points, from lowest to highest. It will also behoove you to memorize this list, since this same group will come back to haunt us in our lesson on *iẓhār*.

The ء and ه are pronounced from the lower throat. When you cough lightly, you are mimicking the sharp, percussive sound of the ء. At the beginning of a syllable, it sounds like the *a* in "<u>a</u>ct," the *oo* in "<u>oo</u>ps," and the *e* in "<u>e</u>ternal." At the end of a word, the percussive sound of the ء comes across almost as an afterthought to the word as in the word سَمَاء.

The ه is articulated from the lower throat. It should be pronounced just like an English *h*, in that its sound is airy, and the vocal cords do not vibrate.[2] However, many professional reciters pronounce the ه with a vibration of the vocal cords more akin to a sigh or a moan than to an *h*. Accordingly, we are justified in pronouncing it either way.

The ع is one of the more challenging letters to pronounce. It is articulated from the middle throat by slightly constricting the

---

[2] One reciter who consistently pronounces the ه in an airy, voiceless way is Maḥmūd Khalīl al-Ḥuṣarī.

throat around the voice box. Its sound is akin to the sound of gagging; however, you must be sure not to cut off the air flow altogether.[3] Because of their difficulty with ع, some people give up and simply pronounce it like a ء. Others (such as many Urdu speakers) try so zealously to constrict their throat that they end up cutting the air off altogether producing a very harsh sound. Both extremes are to be avoided.

The ح is also articulated by slightly constricting the middle throat, in much the same way as we did for ع. This constriction should create a bit of friction in the throat as you exhale deeply as if to fog up your glasses to clean them. Its sound should remind you of an angry goose hissing to keep you at bay. If you pronounce the ح with too little friction it will turn into a ه. Too much friction will make it sound harsh and unnatural, a common mistake among many Urdu speakers.

The غ and خ are both articulated in the same way. They come from the upper throat where it opens into the mouth. You can get your throat into position by pressing the back of your tongue lightly against the uvula (the flesh that hangs down at the back of your mouth). With throat in position, if you exhale using only air, you will produce the خ. And if you use your vocal chords,

[3] One reciter who consistently pronounces the ع correctly is Muḥammad Ṣiddīq al-Minshāwī.

you will produce the غ. These letters are akin to the French *r*. The غ sounds much like the sound of gargling. And the خ sounds like a snore, only the sound comes on the exhale instead of the intake. People with a Persian background are notorious for mixing up غ and ق.

It is important to note that غ and خ are the first two of the "8 thick letters" after which the *fatḥah* and *alif* must be pronounced thickly like the *aw* in "raw" and "thaw."

Group IV – The Deep-tongue Consonants:

ك	ق

These two letters are pronounced at the back of the mouth between the back of the tongue and the back of the soft palette. Let us start with the ك, since it is identical to the *k* and hard *c* in English. To get the ق shift the point of contact between the tongue and palette slightly further back from the ك until you achieve a deep clicking sound. This is the ق.

Many different ethnic groups—including most Arabs—have difficulty pronouncing this letter. Hyderabadis are notorious for pronouncing the ق as a خ. The Egyptians and the Lebanese render it a ء. Saudis and Iraqis make it into a hard *g* sound like a Persian گ. As I mentioned earlier, the Iranians and Afghanis transpose it with the غ. And many English speakers simply equate it with the

ك. I mention these idiosyncrasies in hopes that being aware of them will allow you to avoid them.

Note again that the ق is the third of the "8 thick letters" after which the *fatḥah* and *alif* must be pronounced thickly like the *aw* in "raw" and "thaw."

Group V – The Middle-tongue Consonants:

ي	ش	ج

These letters are pronounced between the middle of the tongue and the middle of the palette. ج is equivalent to the *j* and soft *g* in English. Probably because of their connection with the French, the Lebanese and Syrians incorrectly pronounce this letter like the *g* in "protégé."[4] To avoid this, they should press their tongue firmly against their palette to stop the flow of air and create a hard *j* sound.

The ش is just like the *sh* blend in "ship."

The ي sound is just like the *y* in "yellow." You will notice that this is the second time I have mentioned ي in these lists. When ي has a *sukūn* it acts like a long vowel and belongs in Group I. When it

[4] *Tajwīd* scholars refer to this incorrect pronunciation of ج by the Lebanese and Syrians as *ta'ṭīsh*.

has a short vowel on it, it is a consonant and belongs here in Group V.

Group VI – The Front-tongue consonants:

ن	ل	ر

These three letters are articulated using the tip of the tongue and the ridge of the palette just behind the upper incisors. The ر, unlike the English *r*, must be rolled. However, it is not rolled so copiously as in Spanish and Portuguese. Rather, its roll should be muted.

Note again that the ر is the fourth of the "8 thick letters" after which the *fatḥah* and *alif* must be pronounced thickly like the *aw* in "r<u>aw</u>" and "th<u>aw</u>."

The ل differs from the American *l* in that the former has more energy while the latter is lazier. Well, this is not completely true. Compare the words "<u>l</u>augh" and "be<u>ll</u>." When *l* comes at the beginning of English words, it is crisp like the ل. However, when it comes at the end of syllables, it is rounded and lazy, unlike the ل. To get the crisp sound, use the tip of your tongue, and press it firmly against the palette just behind the upper incisors.

Finally, ن is pronounced just like *n*.

We shall be revisiting this group in greater detail in later chapters as we discuss the "sun" and "moon" letters, the rules for the ل in the word الله , the rules for ر, and the rules for ن with a *sukūn* and ن with a *shaddah*.

Group VII – The Hard Dental Consonants:

ط	ت	د

These three letters are articulated with the tip of the tongue pressed against the base of the upper incisors. The د and ت are pronounced just like *d* and *t*, respectively.

To say the ط, the tip of the tongue should remain in the same position as the ت. The position of the length of the tongue, however, will change. With the ت it is basically flat and horizontal and hits its target head on. For the ط, on the other hand, it must curl upward and hit it from beneath.

Note again that the ط is the fifth of the "8 thick letters" after which the *fatḥah* and *alif* must be pronounced thickly like the *aw* in "r<u>aw</u>" and "th<u>aw</u>."

Group VIII – The Airy Dental Consonants:

ظ	ث	ذ

These three letters are articulated with the tip of the tongue pressed lightly against the tips of the front upper incisors.

The ذ is identical to the *th* blend in "that," "those," and "them." Often, people cannot get this letter to buzz as it must. The trick is to increase the space between the tongue and the incisors and increase the flow of air. You should be able to prolong this buzzing sound indefinitely if you are pronouncing it correctly. People from the Subcontinent often pronounce the *th* in the words above as an aspirated *d* sound. While this is acceptable in the Indian dialect of English, it is not acceptable in Arabic.

The ث is identical to the *th* blend in "thanks" and "think." The same trick applies here that you learned for the ذ, although there is no buzz here. People from the Subcontinent also have a similar problem with this sound whereby they pronounce it as an aspirated *t* sound. Once again they must correct this when they read Arabic.

You can think of the relationship between ذ and ظ to be the same as the relationship between the ت and ط. The tongue in the former in each pair is flat while in the latter it curls upward.

Note again that the ظ is the sixth of the "8 thick letters" after which the *fatḥah* and *alif* must be pronounced thickly like the *a* in "raw" and "thaw."

Group IX – The Whistling Consonants:

ص	ز	س

These three letters are pronounced from a point of articulation close to that of Group V, though their whistling attribute overrides any similarity.

The س is just like *s*, and the ز is just like *z*.

To articulate the ص start with the س, then arch your tongue, and let the middle portion rise toward the palette instead of approaching it horizontally. Thus, the sound of ص is produced entirely by the placement of the tongue, not by moving the lips to the right, an incorrect practice among some Arab reciters.

Note again that the ص is the seventh of the "8 thick letters" after which the *fatḥah* and *alif* must be pronounced thickly like the *aw* in "raw" and "thaw."

Group X - The Nemesis of non-Arabs:

ض

The ض is a letter peculiar to Arabic, for which reason the language is sometimes referred to as *lughat al-ḍād* (the "Language of ض"). It is pronounced by first filling the tongue broadly into the upper palette. The actual sound comes when the right or left edge of the tongue strikes the upper premolars and molars on the same side of the mouth. This means that the sound actually comes out of the side of the mouth, not the front. Unfortunately, many Arabs today mispronounce the ض by using the tip of the tongue instead of the sides. This is to be avoided.

Now that you have understood the point of articulation for ض, I must tell you that there are two acceptable ways to pronounce it. *Tajwīd* scholars mention that ض possesses the attribute of *rikhāwah* (softness), which means that the air ought to flow continuously without complete interruption as the letter is being pronounced. If we implement this attribute, the result is a sound very similar to ظ. In fact many *tajwīd* scholars state explicitly that there is no difference between the sound of ض and ظ except that the former is pronounced with the side of the tongue and the latter is pronounced with the tip of the tongue.[5]

The majority of Qur'ān reciters, however, do not observe this attribute of ض, hence giving us the second way to pronounce it: with the opposite of *rikhāwah*, *shiddah* (hardness). Accordingly, the air flow will completely cease as the ض is being pronounced, giving it a quality distinct from ظ completely.

Note one last time that the ض is the eighth and last of the "8 thick letters" after which the *fatḥah* and *alif* must be pronounced thickly like the *aw* in "raw" and "thaw."

[5] al-Ḥuṣarī, Maḥmūd Khalīl. *Aḥkām qirā'at al-qur'ān al-karīm*. 4th ed. *Al-Maktabah al-Makkiyyah* and *Dār al-Bashā'ir*, 1999. footnotes on pp. 59-64.

The Definite Particle أَل

(Sun Letters and Moon Letters)

As I mentioned earlier, many of the rules of *tajwīd* are linked to the letters of Group VI: ر, ل, and ن. I will address these rules beginning in this chapter.

أَل is the definite particle in Arabic roughly equivalent to the English "the." Arabic grammarians correctly refer to it as *lām al-ta'rīf*. However, it is more commonly called *alif lām*. This is a terrible misnomer, since the letter before the ل is not an *alif*, but a *hamzah*—a *hamzat al-waṣl*, to be exact. Here, I shall refer to it simply as أَل. You can call it what you want.

أَل is pronounced in one of two ways, depending on whether it is followed by a "sun letter" or a "moon letter." The diagram below summarizes these rules.

ٱل + sun letter=>silent ل + *shaddah* on sun letter	Example: ٱلشَّمْس
ٱل + moon letter=>ل pronounced normally	Example: ٱلْقَمَر

Before going forward, let me explain what sun and moon letters are. The 28 letters in the Arabic alphabet are divided into two groups of fourteen, based on each letter's relative nearness or distance from the point of articulation for ل. Generally speaking, those letters whose points of articulation are very close to that of ل are called sun letters because the Arabic word for "sun" is ٱلشَّمْس, which, as we saw above, is the classic example for a sun letter. Those letters whose points of articulation are farther from that of ل are called moon letters because the Arabic word for "moon" is ٱلْقَمَر, which is also the classic example for a moon letter.

The sun letters are:

ت	ث	د	ذ	ر	ز	س	ش	ص	ض	ط	ظ	ل	ن

The moon letters are:

ي	ه	و	م	ك	ق	ف	غ	ع	خ	ح	ج	ب	ء

There is not much need for you to memorize these lists of letters. Nonetheless, if you would like to memorize them, you can use the following mnemonic device to learn the moon letters, and by correlation, the rest will be sun letters:

إِبْغِ حَجَّكَ وَ خَفْ عَقِيمَهُ

Pursue the Ḥajj, and beware of an unsuccessful one.

A more useful pursuit than memorizing this list is to understand the reason why sun and moon letters act differently. This division was not made arbitrarily; rather, for the linguistic reasons at which I hinted earlier: each letter's relative nearness or distance from the point of articulation for ل. In particular, Groups II-IV are moon letters. Groups VI-X are sun letters. Group V is split, with ش as a sun letter and ج and ي as moon letters. The letters of Group I, being vowels, never occur after آل, so they are outside of this classification. The diagram below summarizes this breakdown.

Group	Sun	Moon	Neither
I			All
II-IV		All	
V	ش	ي ج	
VI-X	All		

Because the sun letters' points of articulation are close to that of the ل, it would be difficult, and often awkward, to pronounce both. For this reason, Arabs change the ل into the same letter as the sun letter and then merge the two identical letters. This transformation is marked by writing nothing over the ل and doubling the sun letter. This process can be illustrated as follows:

ٱلْرَعْد ← أَرْرَعْد ← أَرَّعْد (=ٱلرَّعْد)

There is no such difficulty with the moon letters, so the ل is left alone and pronounced normally.

To help you better understand this difference between the sun and moon letters, I will give you one sample word beginning with each letter of the alphabet, preceded by ٱلْ. Experiment by saying each word as though its first letter were a moon letter (since this is the default). You will notice how difficult it is to pronounce the sun letters in this way. You will also notice how easy it is to pronounce the moon letters in this way.

ٱلرَّعْد	ٱلْرَعْد	Group VI
ٱلنَّار	ٱلْنَار	Group VI
ٱللُّبّ	ٱلْلُبّ	Group VI

ٱلتُّرَاب	ٱلْتُرَاب	Group VII
ٱلدَّار	ٱلْدَار	Group VII
ٱلطُّور	ٱلْطُور	Group VII
ٱلثَّرَى	ٱلْثَرَى	Group VIII
ٱلذِّكْر	ٱلْذِكْر	Group VIII
ٱلظَّالِم	ٱلْظَالِم	Group VIII
ٱلسَّيْر	ٱلْسَيْر	Group IX
ٱلزَّكَاة	ٱلْزَكَاة	Group IX
ٱلصَّادِق	ٱلْصَادِق	Group IX
ٱلضَّامِر	ٱلْضَامِر	Group X
ٱلشَّمْس	ٱلْشَمْس	Group V
	ٱلْيَاقُوت	Group V
	ٱلْجَمَل	Group V

	ٱلْفِتْنَة	Group II
	ٱلْوَارِث	Group II
	ٱلْمَوْج	Group II
	ٱلْبَأْس	Group II
	ٱلْأَهْل	Group III
	ٱلْهَادِي	Group III
	ٱلْعَتِيق	Group III
	ٱلْحُبّ	Group III
	ٱلْغَار	Group III
	ٱلْخُشُوع	Group III
	ٱلْكَهْف	Group IV
	ٱلْقَلَم	Group IV

Common Pitfalls

There are certain words that appear to be composed of ٱل plus a sun letter. However, upon closer inspection, we see that they are not.

1) ٱلَّذِي, ٱلَّذِينَ, and ٱلَّتِي

These relative pronouns may look as though they comprise ٱل plus ذ or ت, but they do not. One clue to look for is the *shaddah* on the ل. Had these words comprised ٱل plus a sun letter, the *shaddah* would have been on the sun letter, not the ل.

2) أَلْسِنَة

The *hamzah* on this word is *hamzat al-qaṭ'* and there is no *shaddah* on the س, so it is not ٱل plus a sun letter.

3) ٱلْتَقَى

Here the *hamzah* is *hamzat al-waṣl*, but it is not ٱل. The ل is actually one of this word's root letters.

ل With a *Shaddah*

In chapter one, I mentioned that eight letters are thick and the rest are thin. We shall now amend this statement and see that ل is sometimes thin (pronounced with *tarqīq*) and sometimes thick (pronounced with *tafkhīm*). In particular, when ل occurs in any word other than ٱللَّه and ٱللَّهُمَّ it is categorically pronounced with a thin sound. By this I mean that the *fatḥah* and the *alif* after it should be pronounced like the *a* in attempt and apple, respectively. For example, look at the following words. Whether ل has a short vowel or long vowel, and whether it has a *shaddah* or not, it is thin:

لَمْ
لَا
ٱلَّذِي
أَلَّا

When ل is in the words ٱللَّه and ٱللَّهُمَّ, on the other hand, we have to see what precedes it. If it is preceded by a *fatḥah* or a *ḍammah*, it should be pronounced with a thick sound, meaning the *fatḥah* and the *alif* after it should be pronounced like the vowel sound in the words *law* and *lock*. It does not matter whether the *fatḥah* or *ḍammah* is on the letter directly before the ل or several letters before (as is the case when there are silent letters before the ل) as long as it is on the last letter to be pronounced before the ل. If it is preceded by a *kasrah* it should be pronounced with a thin sound. Look at the following examples:

Thick	بَعَثَ ٱللَّه
Thick	نَرَى ٱللَّه
Thick	يُرِيدُ ٱللَّه
Thick	وَٱسْتَغْفِرُوا۟ ٱللَّه
Thick	سُبْحَانَكَ ٱللَّهُمَّ
Thick	قَالَا ٱللَّهُمَّ
Thick	نَقُولُ ٱللَّهُمَّ
Thick	قَالُوا۟ ٱللَّهُمَّ
Thin	بِسْمِ ٱللَّه
Thin	فِي ٱللَّه
Thin	قُلِ ٱللَّهُمَّ
Thin	قُولِي ٱللَّهُمَّ

Rules for ر

The letter ر is another letter from Group VI that has detailed rules. In chapter one, I included ر among the eight thick letters. We must now delve a little deeper to examine its various circumstances. We shall see that it is sometimes thin (pronounced with *tarqīq*) and sometimes thick (pronounced with *tafkhīm*).

First of all, what does it mean for the ر to be thick and thin? Its thickness and thinness are determined by the shape of our lips as we pronounce it. To make a thick ر, we must pucker our lips as we say ر, as though they are in position for و. To make it thin, we must stretch our lips horizontally as we say it, as if we are smiling broadly.

Broadly speaking, we will use the following thought process to examine any ر that we encounter in our reading. First, we will look at the *ḥarakah* of the ر itself. If it does not have a *ḥarakah* we will look to the letter before the ر. If that too does not have a *ḥarakah* we will look to the *ḥarakah* on the letter before the letter before the ر.

Now, let us look at these rules in detail. If ر has a *ḥarakah*, we will apply the following standards. If it has a *fatḥah* or a *ḍammah*, it will be thick, as in رَبِّي, رَاق, رُزِقَ, and رُوح. If it has a *kasrah*, it will be thin, as in رِزْق and رِيح. Look at the following diagram. The thick ر is red, while the thin ر is green. Notice, also that the ر with a *sukūn* is gray indicating that its ruling has yet to be explained.

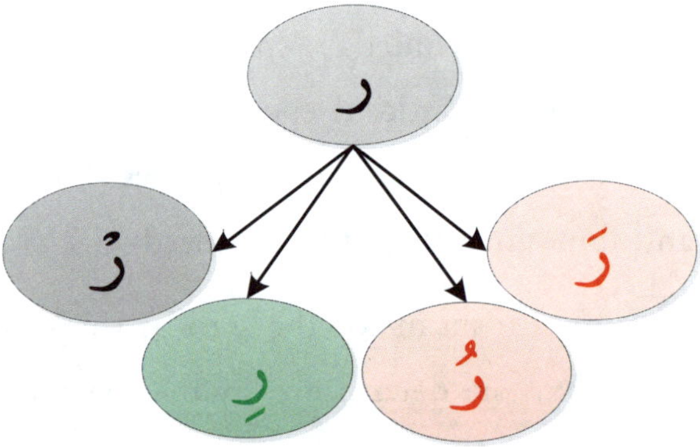

If ر does not have a *ḥarakah* but a *sukūn*, then we must look to the letter before it. If that letter has a *fatḥah* or a *ḍammah*, then the ر will be thick, as in أَكْبَرْ and تُرْجَعُوْن. If that letter has a *kasrah* or a *sukūn* we still have more work to do. Look at the following diagram, and notice that the ر with a *kasrah* and ر with a *sukūn* are gray indicating that their ruling has yet to be explained.

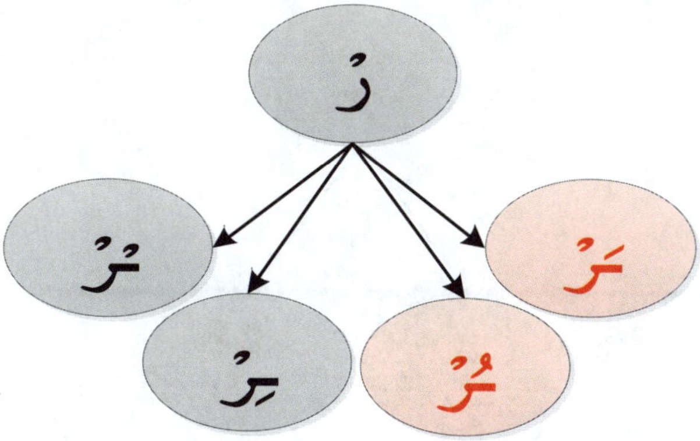

Let us deal first with the ر preceded by a *kasrah*. If this *kasrah* is on a *hamzat al-waṣl*, then the ر is thick, as in فَٱرْجِعُوٓاْ, ٱرْجِعُوٓاْ, and رَبِّ ٱرْجِعُونِ.[6] Look at the following diagram.

---

[6] If you do not know basic Arabic morphology, you might be confused by the second and third examples, since there is apparently no *kasrah* on the *hamzat al-waṣl*. In reality, the *kasrah* has been omitted because the *hamzah* has been omitted in pronunciation. In lieu of teaching you the grammatical rule, let me tell you a secret: When there is a *hamzat al-waṣl* before a ر with a *sukūn*, the ر is *always* thick because, in this case, the *hamzat al-waṣl* can only take a *ḍammah* or a *kasrah* according to the rules of morphology, and in either case it is to be pronounced as a thick letter.

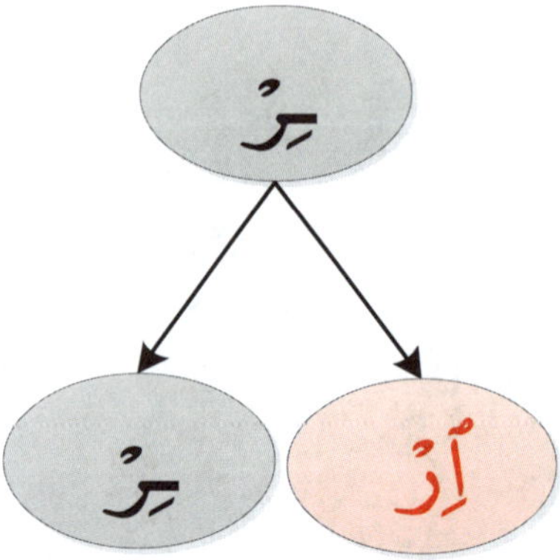

If the *kasrah* is on any other letter besides *hamzat al-waṣl*, then look to the letter after the ر. If that letter is one of the seven remaining thick letters (خص ضطظ غق), then the ر is thick, as in قِرْطَاس, مِرْصَاد, and فِرْقَة. If not, then it is thin, as in فِرْعَوْن, مِرْيَة, and إِرْبَة. Look at the following diagram.

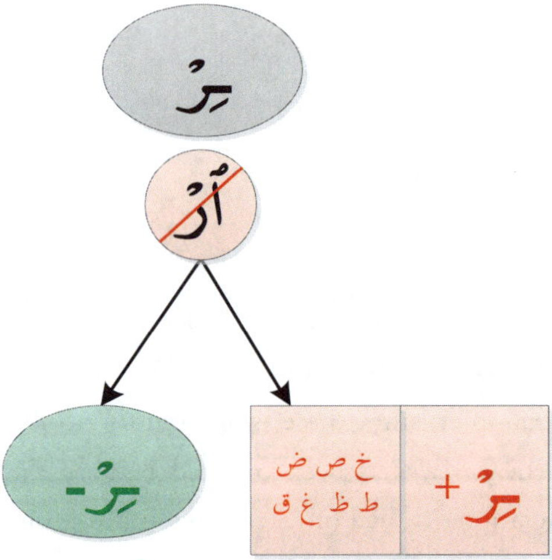

Let us now return to the case of a ر with a *sukūn* preceded by a letter with a *sukūn*. In this case, we must see whether that *sukūn* is on a ي or not. If it is on a ي then the ر is thin, as in خَيْرٌ and بَصِيرٌ. See the following diagram.

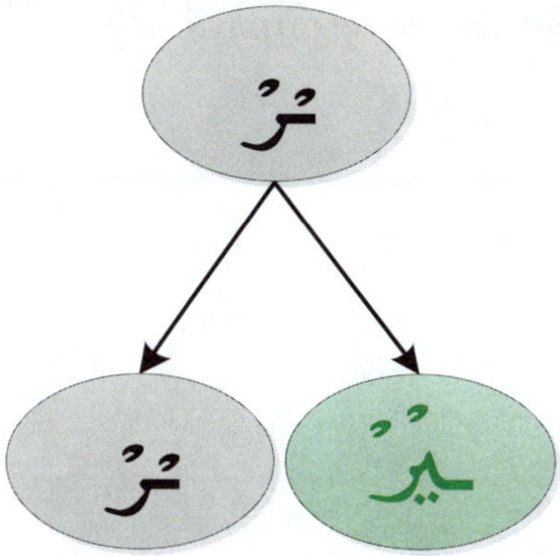

If the *sukūn* is not on a ي, then we must look two letters before the ر, and we will use the same standard we used before for the *ḥarakah* of the ر itself: if the letter has a *fatḥah* or a *ḍammah*, then the ر is thick, as in صَبْرٌ and عُسْرٌ. If it has a *kasrah*, the ر is thin, as in ذِكْرٌ. See the following diagram.

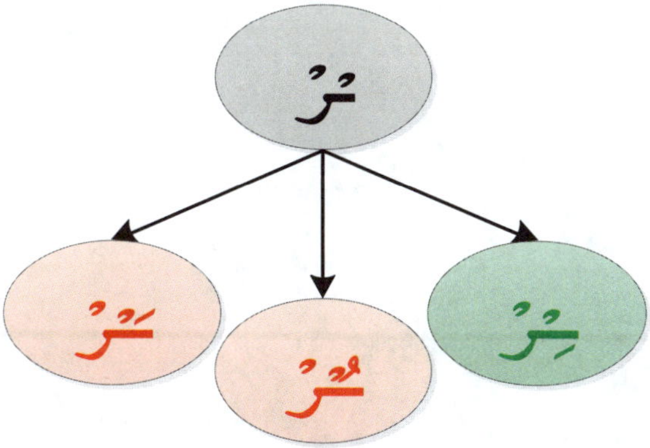

I know these rules sound mindboggling at first. However, with the help of the following chart, and with plenty of practice, you will be able to make these determinations on the fly as you read.

Rules for ن with a *Sukūn*

The final letter from Group VI that we must tackle is ن, in particular *nūn sākinah* (*nūn* with a *sukūn*). When we speak of *nūn sākinah* we are really speaking of two apparently different forms. The obvious form of *nūn sākinah* is نْ. The form that may not be so familiar to you is the *tanwīn*. Both are essentially *nūn sākinah* as I indicate in the following diagram.

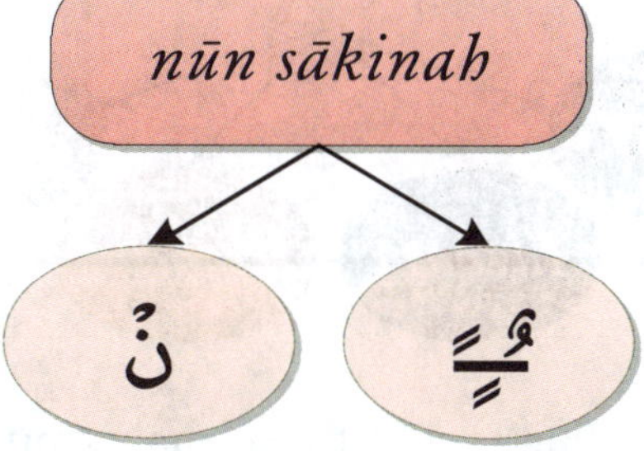

To demonstrate that *tanwīn* is indeed a form of *nūn sākinah*, we can rewrite the *tanwīn* as in the following diagram.

Tanwīn = نْ

كِتَابَنْ = كِتَاباً

كِتَابُنْ = كِتَابٌ

كِتَابِنْ = كِتَابٍ

Thus, whenever you see a *tanwīn* you can rewrite it in your mind as a *nūn sākinah*. It follows that all the rules that we cover in this chapter for *nūn sākinah* are equally applicable to the *tanwīn*.

Nūn sākinah is pronounced in one of four ways depending on the letter that immediately follows it. It will either be pronounced with *iẓhār*, *idghām*, *iqlāb*, or *ikhfā'* as in the diagram below.

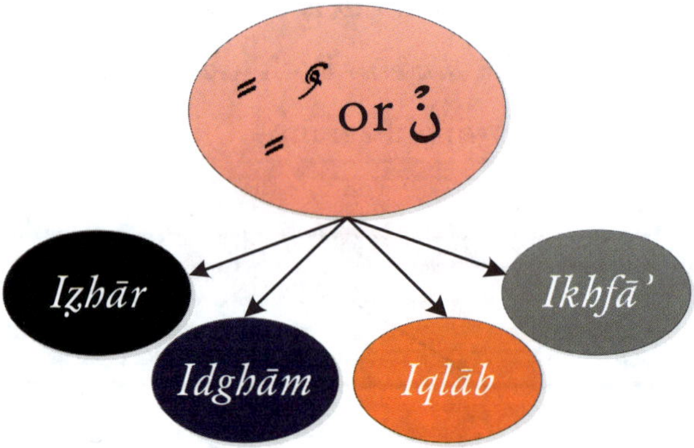

Let us first divide the letters of the alphabet into four groups and then identify which rule applies to *nūn sākinah* in each circumstance.

Iẓhār

(expressing the نْ clearly)

When *nūn sākinah* is followed by any of the letters from Group III, the throat letters, it will be pronounced with *iẓhār*. To do *iẓhār* of the *nūn sākinah* is to express the *nūn* clearly from its point of articulation as you would have done had you not read this chapter. The reason the *nūn sākinah* is expressed clearly when followed by the throat letters is that their points of articulation are far enough away that they do not hinder the pronunciation of the *nūn*. The following diagram summarizes the formula for *iẓhār*:

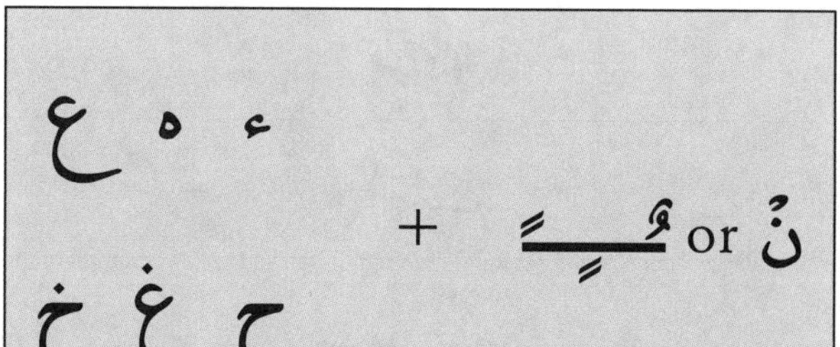

In the calligrapher ʿUthmān Ṭāhā's convention, there is a special shorthand to indicate *iẓhār*. On the نْ you will find a symbol derived from the head of the letter خ. It is a *sukūn*, but its shape is derived from the خ as an abbreviation for خَفِيف, meaning "light." Whenever you see this symbol—on a ن or any other letter—it indicates *iẓhār*. *Iẓhār* of a *tanwīn* is indicated by its vertical alignment. The following diagram summarizes these shorthands.

'Uthmān Ṭā Ḥā shorthand for Iẓhār

نْ or ـٌـٍـً

If you peak ahead to *idghām* and *ikhfā'*, and compare the *tanwīns* here and there, you will see what I mean when I say the *tanwīns* for *iẓhār* are vertically aligned. Some examples of *iẓhār* are:

مِنْ إِلَهٍ
أَنْعَمْتَ
عَزِيزٌ غَفُور
رِزْقًا حَسَنًا

Idghām

(merging the نْ)

When *nūn sākinah* is followed by any of the letters from the mnemonic يَرْمَلُون, we will do *idghām* of the ن into that letter. *Idghām* means to merge one sound into the other. The general formula for *idghām* is as follows:

يَرْمَلُون + ـًـٍـٌ or ن

Before we look at the details of *idghām*, we must divide these six letters into يُومِن and لَرْ. The letters of يُومِن are special because the ن keeps its quality of *ghunnah* when merging into them. *Ghunnah* is the nasal sound characteristic of ن and م, which are the only two letters whose sounds come entirely through the nose. In short, the *idghām* of ن into يُومِن maintains this nasal sound, while the *idghām* of ن into لَرْ does not. See the following diagram:

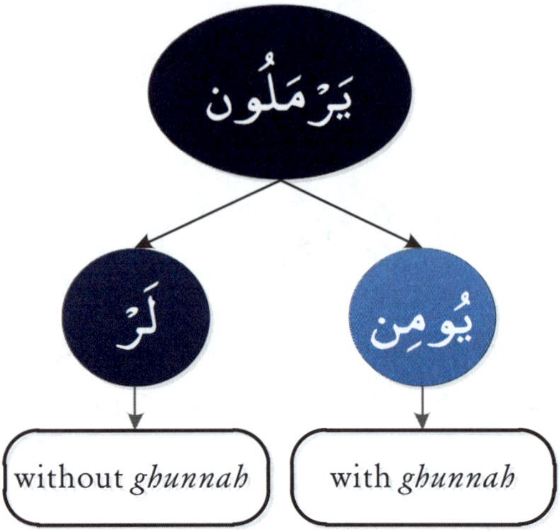

We can further divide يَرْمَلُون into يُو, مِن, and لَر based on whether the *idghām* of ن into these letters is complete or partial. In complete *idghām*, the ن is so thoroughly merged with the other letter that it is lost altogether, and no sign of the ن remains in pronunciation. This happens in the case of مِن and لَر. We can make sense of this rule by realizing that the letters ل, ر, and ن share the same point of articulation with ن, thus making it easier to completely merge one into the other than to do acrobatics of the tongue to pronounce both. While م is not part of the same group, it shares with ن the essential quality of *ghunnah*, as I just mentioned, thus making it very awkward to transition from one to the other.

In partial *idghām* on the other hand, the nasal sound of the ن remains even as the و and ي are pronounced, yielding a twangy sound unlike anything in English. The following diagram shows instances of partial and complete *idghām* and indicates the presence or absence of *ghunnah*.

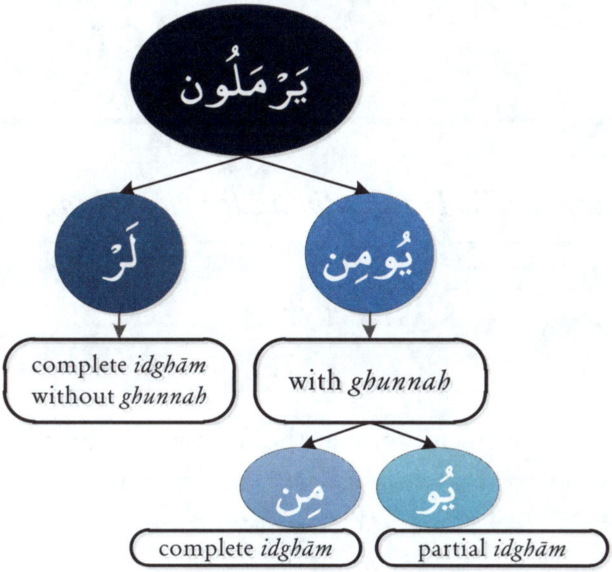

It is important to note that in all four cases of *idghām* with *ghunnah*, we must accentuate the nasalization and stretch the sound for the duration of two *ḥarakahs* (like a *madd ṭabīʿī*, which will be discussed in more detail in the chapter on "*madd*").

The ʿUthmān Ṭāhā convention indicates *idghām* by putting nothing over the ن and by shifting the *tanwīns* so they are not vertically aligned. If the *idghām* is complete, it indicates this by putting a *shaddah* over the following letter, indicating that you skip the ن altogether.

ʿUthmān Ṭā Ḥā shorthand for complete idghām

ـّ	+	ـً ـٌ ـٍ	or	ن

ʿUthmān Ṭā Ḥā shorthand for partial idghām

ـً ـٌ ـٍ	or	ن

Keeping all this in mind, look at the following examples:

وَلَمْ يَكُن لَّهُۥ
خَيْرٌ لِّلَّذِينَ
مِن رَّبِّهِمْ
مُّحَمَّدٌ رَّسُولُ ٱللَّهِ
وَإِن يَرَوْا۟
خَيْرًا يَرَهُۥ
مِن وَالٍ

يَوْمَئِذٍ وَاجِفَةٌ
مِن مِّثْلِهِ
صِرَاطاً مُّسْتَقِيماً
مِن نَّصِيرٍ
حِطَّةٌ نَّغْفِرْ

Additionally it is important to note that *idghām* of the ن only occurs at the end of words, never in the middle. For this reason, we do not do *idghām* in the following words:

دُنْيَا
قِنْوَان
صِنْوَان
بُنْيَان

Finally, in some instances where we are meant to pause briefly, a small س will be placed at the end of the word, indicating a *sakt*, or pause. This pause will prevent us from doing *idghām*. Below is one instance of the *sakt*:

مَنْۜ رَاقٍ

Iqlāb

(changing the نْ to م)

When *nūn sākinah* is followed by a ب, we will pronounce it with *iqlāb*. *Iqlāb* means to change something. Here we will change the ن into a م to make it easier to pronounce before the ب. It is not quite that simple though. When we change the ن into a م, we will then enact another rule called *ikhfā' shafawī*. To do this, you must not quite close your lips on the م, rather allow them to hover just short of touching until you get to the ب. It is important to note that, since the letter م is involved, there is a *ghunnah*, and we must accentuate this nasalization. We will do this by stretching the sound for the duration of two *ḥarakahs* (like we did for the *idghām* with *ghunnah*).

The following diagram summarizes the formula for *iqlāb*.

ب	+	ـًـٍـٌ	or	نْ

The ʿUthmān Ṭāhā convention indicates *iqlāb* with a small ۢ in place of a *sukūn* over the ن or in place of one of the *ḥarakah*s. See the following diagram.

ʿUthmān Ṭā Ḥā shorthand for Iqlāb

ـَۢ	ـِۭ	ـُۢ	or	نۢ

The following are examples of *iqlāb*:

أَنۢبِيَاء
مِنۢ بَعۡدِ
سَمِيعَۢا بَصِيرٗا

Ikhfā'

(hiding the نْ)

When *nūn sākinah* is followed by any letter not in the three groups we have already discussed, we will pronounce it with *ikhfā'*. *Ikhfā'* means to conceal something. Here we shall conceal the sound of the ن in the letter that follows it. To do this, we must not let our tongue and palette make contact as we did with *iẓhār*. Rather, we must produce the nasal sound of the ن while getting the mouth in position to pronounce the next letter. Once again, because we are dealing with *ghunnah* here, we must accentuate the nasalization and stretch the sound for the duration of two *ḥarakahs* (as we did for *idghām* with *ghunnah* and *iqlāb*).

The following diagram summarizes the rule for *ikhfā'*.

Any other letter	+	ـً ـٌ / ـٍ	or	نْ

In the ʿUthmān Ṭāhā convention, *ikhfā'* looks just like partial *idghām*, which is justifiable, since it is similar to partial *idghām* in that the ن is somewhat blended into the letter that follows it. However, this makes it difficult for the beginner to discern the circumstances for each rule. For this reason, we cannot rely solely on the shorthands, but must memorize and recognize the groups of letters that cause each rule. The following are two examples of *ikhfā'*:

أَنتَ
مِن دُون

Other Instances of *Idghām*

We have learned about *idghām* in the context of *nūn sākinah*. This is not the only instance of *idghām* in the Qur'ān. In fact, *idghām* is a far reaching rule in Arabic morphology that entails much more than what is relevant to *tajwīd*. You will even find that our jurists use the term *idghām* to refer to the rule for ألْ when it is followed by a sun letter and to refer to *ikhfā'* and *iqlāb*.[7] In this chapter, we will expand our view of *idghām* slightly, to include more than just the rules for *nūn sākinah* when followed by يرملون, but not so much as our jurists and scholars of grammar do.

We have already learned that *idghām* means to merge one letter into another. We have also seen that this merging is sometimes

[7] Al-Sīstānī, 'Alī. *Minhāj al-ṣāliḥīn*. vol. 1, p. 208, issue 611

partial and sometimes complete. Generally speaking, the following four conditions must be met for us to do *idghām* of one letter into another:

1. the two letters must be identical or similar
2. the two letters must be next to each other
3. the two letters must be in a single word or across two words
4. the first letter must have a *sukūn* and the second, a *ḥarakah*

When the conditions for *idghām* are fulfilled, we will do *idghām* of one letter into the other, either completely or partially, depending on the points of articulation and qualities of the two letters.

Before we determine where *idghām* is complete and where it is partial, let us divide *idghām* into its three types: *idghām al-mutamāthilayn, idghām al-mutajānisayn,* and *idghām al-mutaqāribayn* as in the following diagram:

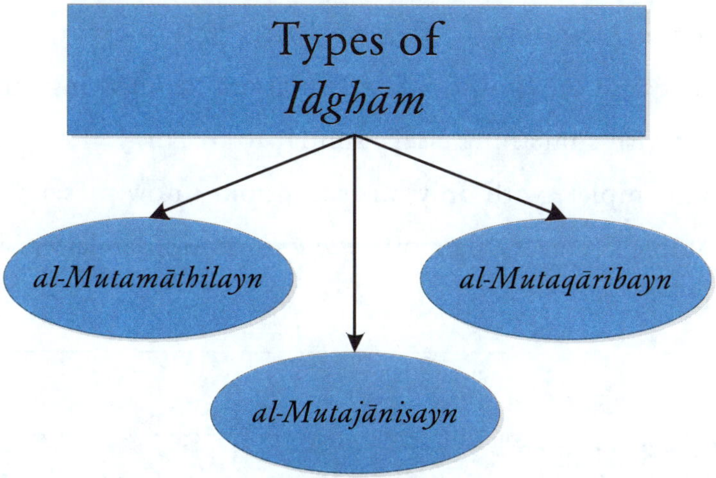

In *idghām al-mutamāthilayn*, the two letters are identical, hence the name. Something that is *mutamāthil* with something else is just like it. This kind of *idghām* is always complete. The *'Uthmān Ṭāhā* convention indicates complete *idghām* with nothing on the first letter and a *shaddah* on the second. Note the following three examples of *idghām al-mutamāthilayn*:

Two identical letters in a single word	يُدۡرِكُّم	=	يُدۡرِككُّمۡ
Two identical letters across two words	لَمۡ تَسۡتَطِعَّلَيۡهِ	=	لَمۡ تَسۡتَطِعۡ عَّلَيۡهِ
Two identical letters across two words. I mention this example to remind you that *idghām* of *nūn sākinah* into ن is *idghām al-mutamāthilayn*	مِنَّصِيرٍ	=	مِن نَّصِيرٍ

In *idghām al-mutajānisayn*, the two letters are different, but they share a common point of articulation. Something that is *mutajānis* with something else is similar to it. This kind of *idghām* is always complete with only one exception. I now present to you one example for every pair of *mutajānis* or similar letters in the Qur'ān.

عَبَدتُّمْ	=	عَبَتُّمْ
أُجِيبَت دَّعْوَتُكُمَا	=	أُجِيبَدَّعْوَتُكُمَا
وَدَّت طَّآئِفَةٌ	=	وَدَّطَّآئِفَةٌ
بَسَطتَ فَرَّطتُمْ		
إِذ ظَّلَمُوٓاْ	=	إِظَّلَمُوٓاْ
يَلْهَث ذَّٰلِكَ	=	يَلْهَذَّٰلِكَ
ٱرْكَب مَّعَنَا	=	ٱرْكَمَّعَنَا
لَمْ يَكُن لَّهُ	=	لَمْ يَكُلَّهُ
مِن رَّبِّهِمْ	=	مِرَّبِّهِمْ

You will notice that I did not give an equivalent for the examples of ط followed by ت. This *idghām* is partial as indicated by the lack of a *shaddah* on the ت. Accordingly, we must pronounce both letters as though the front end of the sound is a ط and the back end is a ت.

It is also worth noting that the last two examples لَمۡ يَكُن لَّهُ and مِن رَّبِّهِمۡ are examples for *idghām* of *nūn sākinah* into لَـرْ, which we discussed in the last chapter.

In *idghām al-mutaqāribayn*, the two letters are different, but their points of articulation are close or they share certain attributes. Something that is *mutaqārib* with something else is literally "close" to it. This kind of *idghām* can be either complete or partial. See the following examples:

points of articulation close	أَلَمۡ نَخۡلُكُّمۡ	=	أَلَمۡ نَخۡلُقكُّمۡ
shared attributes	مِمِّثۡلِهِ	=	مِن مِّثۡلِهِ
points of articulation close			وَإِن يَرَوۡاْ
points of articulation close			مِن وَالٍ

Again, you will notice that we have seen the last three examples in the discussion on *idghām* of the *nūn sākinah* into م, ي, and و.

This division is interesting for those who like to know the inner workings of the language. For those who are not interested or are unable to correctly identify the relationships between letters, there is great news. With the ʿUthmān Ṭāhā convention, all you must do is recognize the notation for complete and partial *idghām*. Once you identify an instance of *idghām* as complete, you will omit the first letter and pronounce the second one with a *shaddah* regardless of the type of *idghām* it is. This leaves only the three instances of partial *idghām*, two of which we discussed in the last chapter. In short, *idghām* is not as difficult as it may at first seem.

Rules for *Madd*

The word *madd* means "to elongate" something. In *tajwīd* it refers to any vowel sound longer than the duration of one *ḥarakah*. If you think of the length of the *ḥarakah* as a unit of time measure, a *madd* is going to be twice to six times as long as that unit, depending on the kind of *madd* and, in some cases, the personal choice of the reciter. Think of the *ḥarakah* as an eighth note in music notation. Whatever the tempo of the piece, the eighth note will be half a beat. The quarter note (which is similar to the *madd ṭabī'ī*) is equal to two eighth notes (or two *ḥarakahs*). And so forth up to the dotted half note (which is equal to the *madd muttaṣil* and *madd lāzim*).

There are basically two types of *madd*. The first occurs whenever the letters from group I (ا, و, and ي) have a *sukūn* on them. The second involves the pronoun ه, which we shall discuss separately at the end of this chapter.

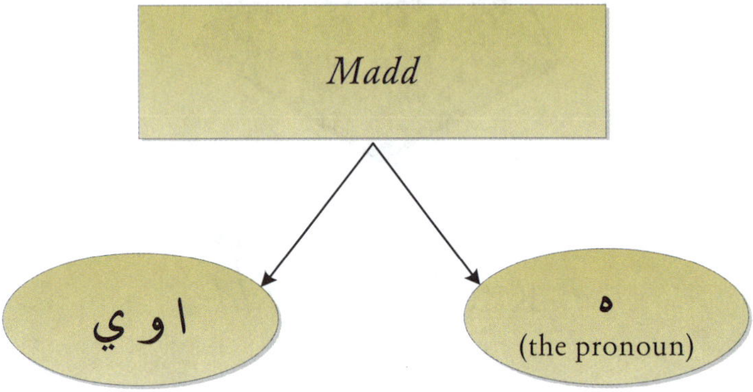

Let us deal first with the long vowels with a *sukūn*. Our first division of the long vowels is based on the *ḥarakah* on the letter before them. Sometimes the *ḥarakah* agrees with the long vowel, meaning there is a *fatḥah* before the ا, a *ḍammah* before the و, and a *kasrah* before the ي. Other times, this is not the case. See the diagram below.

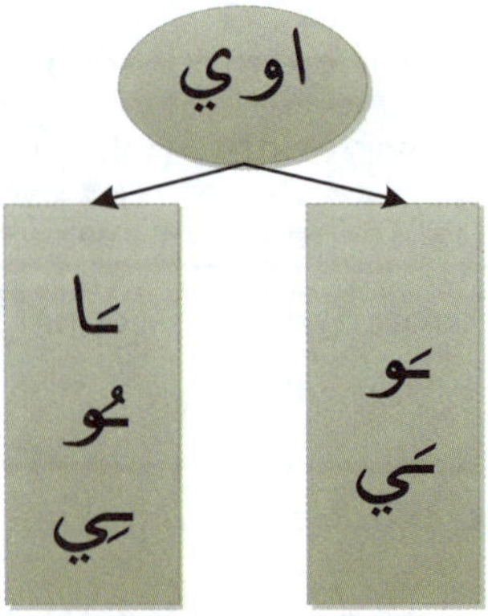

Let us zoom into the group on the left, where the *ḥarakah* agrees with the long vowel. We must next look at what follows the long vowel. The long vowel can either be followed by a ء, by a letter with a *sukūn*, or by neither.

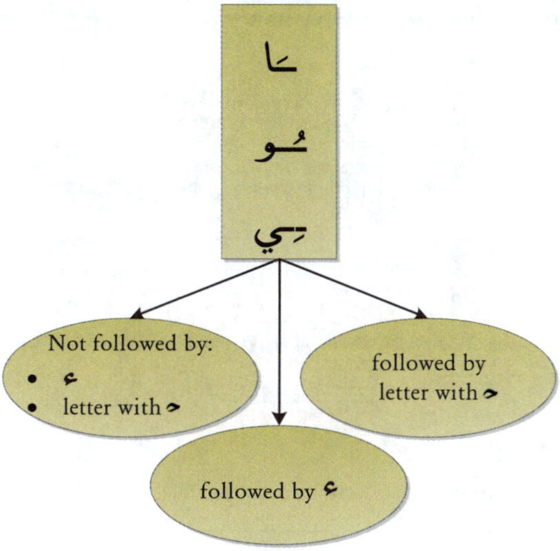

Madd Ṭabīʿī

If the long vowel is followed by neither a ء nor a letter with a *sukūn*, we will call it a *madd ṭabīʿī*, a natural elongation of the vowel, appropriately named because it is natural. Until now, you may not have even thought of such a scenario as being a *madd*, since the conventions of writing the text of the Qurʾān do not write a *madd* symbol (~) over it. It is, nonetheless, a *madd*, a natural *madd*. We will stretch its sound for the length of 2 *ḥarakahs*. To go back to our music analogy, the *madd ṭabīʿī* is like a quarter note, which is equivalent to two eighth notes. We can summarize the *madd ṭabīʿī* as follows:

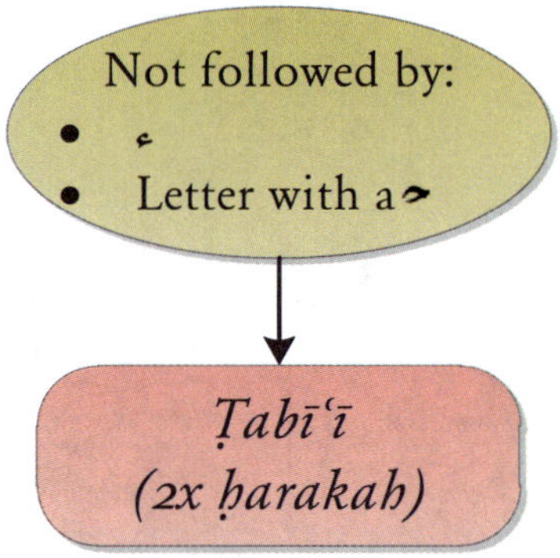

The following are examples of *madd ṭabīʿī*:

قَالَ
يَقُولُ
قِيلَ
قُلنَا

You will notice in each example that the long vowel is followed by neither a ء nor a letter with a *sukūn*. In fact in the fourth example, it is followed by nothing at all.

Madd Muttaṣil & Madd Munfaṣil

If the long vowel is followed by a ء, then there are two scenarios: the ء could be in the same word as the long vowel or in a second word. The former is call *madd muttaṣil,* indicating that the vowel and the ء are "connected" within one word. The latter is called *madd munfaṣil,* indicating that the vowel and the ء are "separated" by a space between the two words. The following diagram summarizes the difference between these two *madds* and each one's degree of elongation. You see a range given because it is upon you as the reciter to decide how long you wish to stretch each one. The only rule here is that you be consistent with each kind of *madd,* so if you stretch your *madd muttaṣil* to 6 counts, make sure you do this for all instances of *madd muttaṣil,* and make sure your *madd munfaṣils* are consistently shorter than *madd muttaṣil.*

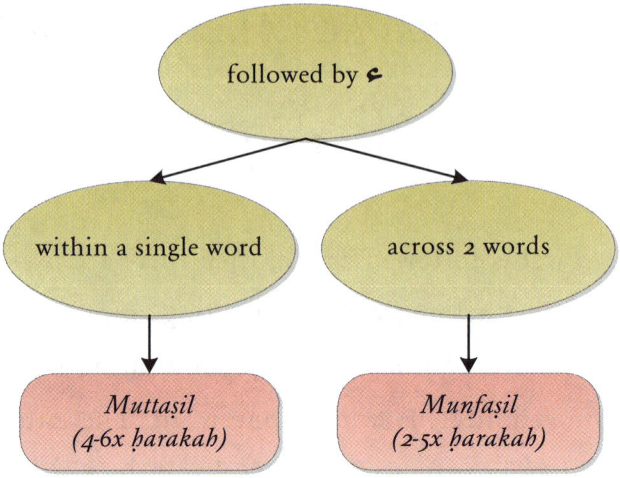

Let us now look at some examples of *madd muttaṣil*:

السَّمَآء
قُرُوٓء
هَنِيٓـًٔا

And let us look at some examples of *madd munfaṣil*:

إِنَّآ أَنزَلۡنَاهُ
قُوٓاْ أَنفُسَكُمۡ
فِيٓ أَنفُسِكُمۡ

In the Qur'ān you will notice that these kinds of *madd* have a wavy line over them that looks like this: ٓ . We tend to call this wavy line a *madd*, when in reality it is the long vowel that is the *madd.* The wavy line is only a sign used to indicate a *madd* that is longer than the *madd ṭabī'ī.* It is interesting that the particular symbol that we use to indicate a *madd* is itself derived from the word مد. If I write it as مـــد and you use your imagination, you should be able to see how the wavy line is a stylized version of this word.

Madd Lāzim & Madd 'Āriḍ

If the long vowel is followed by a *sukūn*, we also have two scenarios: the *sukūn* could be permanent or incidental. By permanent I mean to say that the *sukūn* is actually there, it is actually written. An incidental *sukūn*, on the other hand, is never written as such. Rather, we create a virtual *sukūn* when we choose to stop at the end of verses or anywhere else, in which case we change the ending *ḥarakah* into a *sukūn* in our heads. This is what I mean by an "incidental" *sukūn*, and by contrast, it should now be clear what a "permanent" *sukūn* is.

To get back to the division of the *madd*, if the long vowel is followed by a permanent *sukūn*, it is called *madd lāzim*, because it is "permanently" a *madd* and it is not dependent on your incidental stopping. If it is followed by an incidental *sukūn*, it is called *madd 'āriḍ*, "*'āriḍ*" being the word for incidental. The following diagram summarizes the difference between these two *madds* and each one's degree of elongation.

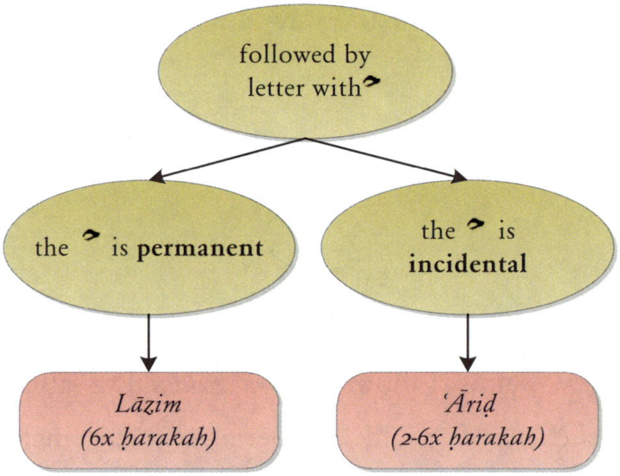

While *madd 'āriḍ* has no further divisions, there are two useful divisions of the *madd lāzim*. First, the long vowel and *sukūn* could be within a word or they could be within a single letter. Before you get too surprised about having a long vowel and a *sukūn* within a *single* letter, let me explain what I mean. I am talking about the *ḥurūf muqaṭṭa'ah*, those letters like الٓمٓ that come at the beginning of some of the Qur'ān's chapters. When we read these letters, we say the names of the letters, which are themselves three letter words. For instance, we say, "*alif lām mīm.*" Let me rewrite these letters like this: أَلِفْ لَامْ مِّيمْ. Now it should be clear that the long vowel in لَامْ is followed by a permanent *sukūn*, as is the vowel in مِّيمْ. The ruling for *madd lāzim* is the same, whether it occurs within a word (*kalimah*), in which case it is called *kalimī*, or within one letter (*ḥarf*), in which case it is called *ḥarfī*. The following diagram summarizes this first division:

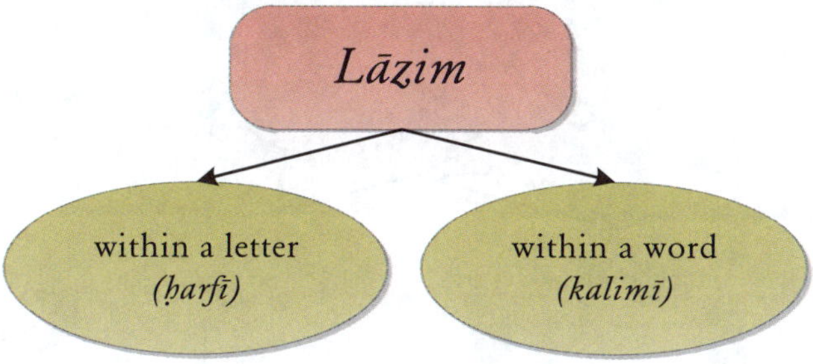

In the second division of *madd lāzim*, we evaluate whether the *sukūn* is part of a *mushaddad* or doubled letter or not. Let me explain. Look at the word ضَالِّينَ. If we break the doubled letter down into its component parts, we can rewrite the word as ضَالْلِينَ. When it is written like this, it is easy to see the long vowel ا followed by a letter with *sukūn*. In fact whenever a long vowel is followed by a letter with a *shaddah*, we have an instance of *madd lāzim*. We call it *muthaqqal*, indicating that it is "heavy" because of the doubling. If on the other hand, there is no *shaddah* involved, like in the word ءَالْـَٔانَ, then we call it *mukhaffaf*, indicating that it is "light" and lacking a heavy *shaddah*. We can apply the same division to the *ḥarfī madd lāzim*. In الٓمٓ (أَلِفْ لَامْ مِّيمْ),

we have a long vowel in لَام that is followed by a م with a *shaddah*, so the *madd* is *muthaqqal*. In قٓ (قَافْ), there is no *shaddah*, and hence the *madd* is *mukhaffaf*. If we combine these two divisions of *madd lāzim*, we end up with four kinds of *madd lāzim*: *ḥarfī muthaqqal*, *ḥarfī mukhaffaf*, *kalimī muthaqqal*, and *kalimī mukhaffaf*. The following two diagrams summarize these divisions:

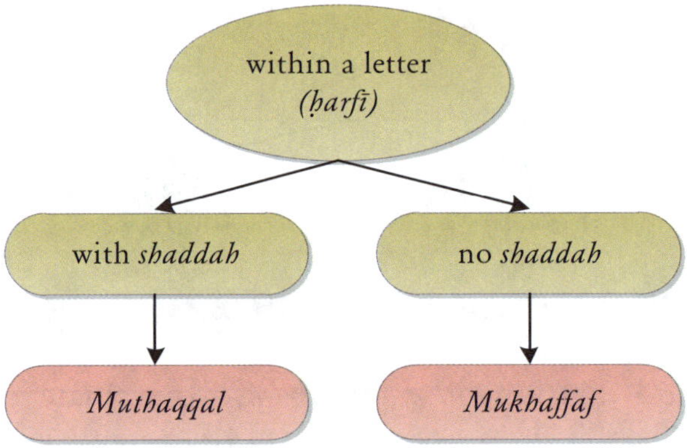

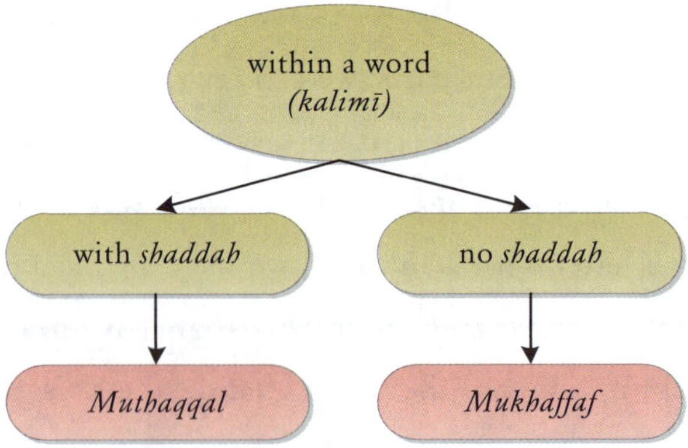

Before we move to the next kind of *madd*, let me give you some examples of *madd ʿāriḍ*, which I defined earlier. Look at the last word of each verse below.

بِسْمِ ٱللَّهِ ٱلرَّحْمَٰنِ ٱلرَّحِيمِ

ٱلْحَمْدُ لِلَّهِ رَبِّ ٱلْعَٰلَمِينَ

ٱلرَّحْمَٰنِ ٱلرَّحِيمِ

You might wonder to what *madd* I am referring, since all you see at the ends of these verses are instances of *madd ṭabīʿī*, and there are no *sukūn*s in sight. That is the nature of *madd ʿāriḍ*: there is no *sukūn* written. Rather, when you decide to stop at the end of a verse or anywhere else, you convert the last *ḥarakah* into a *sukūn* in your mind; hence the *madd ʿāriḍ*. It follows that if you choose to continue from verse one to two or from verse two to three, then you keep the *ḥarakah* and pronounce it as *madd ṭabīʿī*.

Madd Līn

Let me remind you of the following diagram, which I showed you earlier:

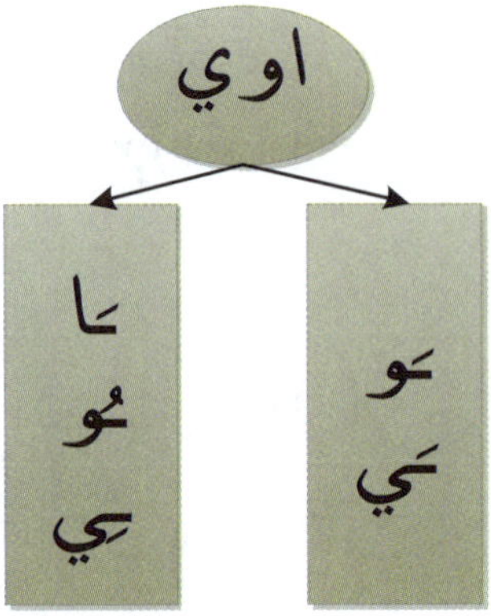

We have now successfully explored all the different *madd*s that stem from the situation on the left where the *ḥarakah* before the long vowel corresponds to the long vowel. Let us now zoom into the column on the right. Whenever a و or ي has a *sukūn*, and is preceded by a *fatḥah*, we have what is called *madd līn* or a "soft" *madd*. This combination of sounds gives us a diphthong where the beginning of the sound is like a *fatḥah* and the end of it is like a و or ي like in the words قُرَيْش and خَوْف. The following diagram summarizes the *madd līn*:

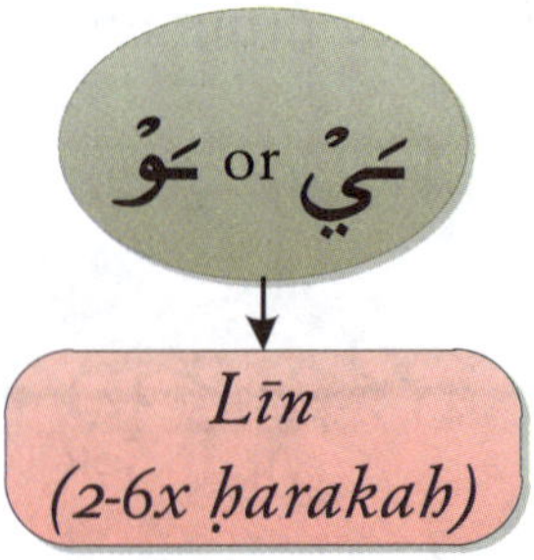

Madd al-Ṣilah

The last kind of *madd* that we must learn is called *madd al-ṣilah*. Let me remind you of the following diagram I showed you at the beginning of this chapter:

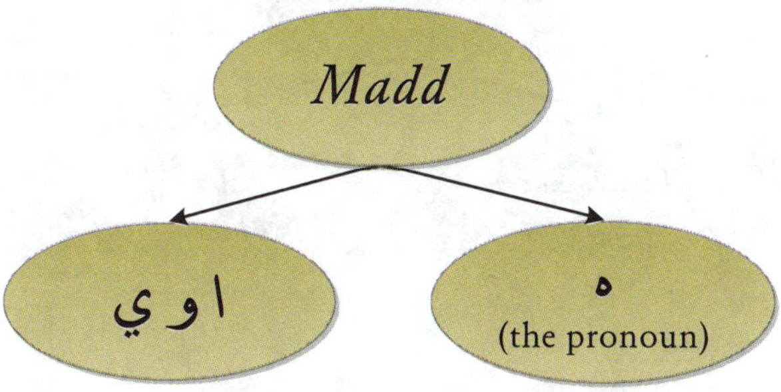

All the *madds* we have discussed until now have related to the long vowels on the left side of this diagram. The *madd al-ṣilah* relates to the singular masculine pronoun ه on the right. This *madd* is likely called *madd al-ṣilah* because the pronoun is considered a thing "attached" or "connected" to the word, which is precisely the meaning of *ṣilah*. This *madd* comes into play whenever the pronoun ه is preceded by a letter with a *ḥarakah*. When this happens, you will simply stretch the *ḥarakah* on the ه using either a و or a ي depending on whether the *ḥarakah* on the ه is a *ḍammah* or *kasrah*, respectively. How long you stretch it depends on whether or not it is followed by a ء in the next word.

If it is not followed by a ء we call it *ṣughrā*, because it is relatively shorter and hence "lesser," and we will only stretch it as long as a *madd ṭabīʿī*. If it is followed by a ء, we call it *kubrā*, because it is relatively longer and hence "greater," and we will stretch it as long as a *madd munfaṣil*. The following diagram summarizes all this information:

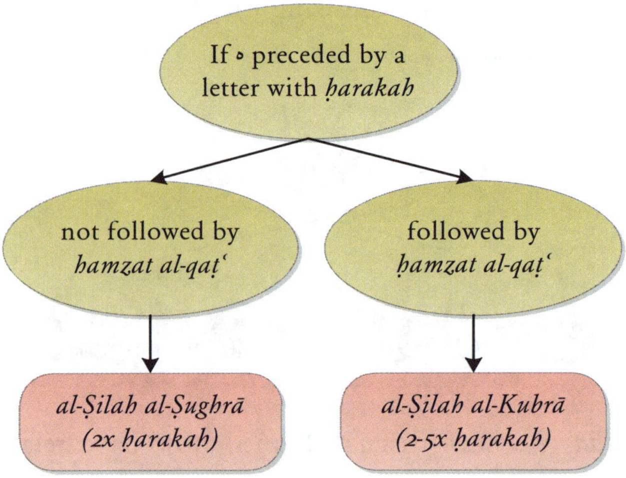

Fortunately, there is a shorthand in the ʿUthmān Ṭāhā convention for both the *ṣilah ṣughrā* and the *ṣilah kubrā*. For the *ṣilah ṣughrā* you will see a small و or ي written after the ه as in the following diagram:

ʿUthmān Ṭā Ḥā shorthand for *Madd al-Ṣilah*

a small و or ۦ

For the *ṣilah kubrā* you will see one of these same two symbols with a ~ over it. The table below contains examples of each kind of *madd al-ṣilah*.

madd al-ṣilah al-ṣughrā	وَرَآءَهُۥ وَهُوَ ٱلْحَق	مِن فَوْقِهِۦ سَحَاب
madd al-ṣilah al-kubrā	وَلَهُۥٓ أَخ	وَمِنْ ءَايَاتِهِۦٓ أَن

Rules for م with a *Sukūn*

The pronunciation of مْ with a *sukūn* depends on the letter that follows it as in the following diagram:

Rules for مْ

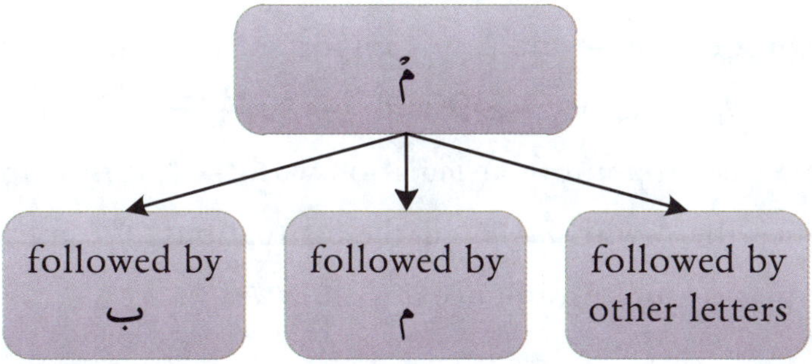

If م is followed by a ب as in وَمَاهُم بِمُؤمِنِينَ, we pronounce it with *ikhfā' shafawī*, which you may recall from our discussion on *iqlāb*. To do this, you must not quite close your lips on the مْ; rather, allow them to hover just short of touching until you get to the ب.

If the مْ with a *sukūn* is followed by another مْ as in فِي قُلُوبِهِم مَّرَض then we have all the conditions for *idghām al-mutamāthilayn* (the merger of two identical letters), which is a complete *idghām* as indicated by the *shaddah* on the second مْ. In this case, because the *idghām* involves a letter pronounced on the lips, we call it *idghām shafawī* (merger on the lips). In the case of *ikhfā' shafawī* and *idghām shafawī* the م must be pronounced with *ghunnah*, which we must stretch for the duration of two *ḥarakahs* (as we did for *idghām* with *ghunnah* and *iqlāb*).

If the مْ with a *sukūn* is followed by anything else, we pronounce it normally and we will call it *iẓhār shafawī*. The sign of this is the *sukūn* on the مْ. While *iẓhār shafawī* occurs when the مْ is followed by *all* letters except ب and مْ, it is important to point it out in the following two examples: هُمْ فِيهَا and أَيمَانَهُمْ وَهَمُّوا. Because the ف and the و share a point of articulation with the مْ, it is tempting to pronounce the مْ with *ikhfā'* in these situations. We must resist this temptation and pronounce it with *iẓhār*.

Rule for م and ن with a *Shaddah*

As we mentioned before, a characteristic exclusive to the letters م and ن is *ghunnah.* In other words, م and ن are the only two letters whose sounds come entirely through the nose. Whenever these two letters have a *shaddah* we must accentuate this nasalization and stretch the sound for the duration of two *ḥarakahs* (like a *madd ṭabīʿī*).

Qalqalah

Qalqalah is a rule to be enacted whenever any of the five letters of the mnemonic قُطْبُ جَدٍّ has a *sukūn*. If it were not for *qalqalah,* these five letters would tend to get obscured whenever they are pronounced with a *sukūn*. To alleviate this problem, we bounce on them ever so slightly, giving them a slight semblance of a *ḥarakah*. That said, we must be wary not to give these letters a full *ḥarakah*, a common mistake, even among reciters. There is no special notation to remind you of *qalqalah*, so you have to be alert. The following are examples where you must enact *qalqalah*:

بِقَلْبِهَا
وَأَطْهَرُ
فَٱرْغَبْ
وَجْهُ ٱللَّهِ
تَدْرُسُونَ

Tas·hīl

(التسهيل)

Tas·hīl literally means to make something *sahl* or "easy." In *tajwīd* it refers to the fudging of the second *hamzah* in the phrase, ءَا۬عۡجَمِيّٞ وَعَرَبِيّٞ in 41:44. Because the ء is a very harsh letter, this particular combination of two *hamzahs* proves to be difficult to pronounce. Accordingly, reciters will often pronounce the second *hamzah* as a hybrid between *hamzah* and *alif*. The notation for *tas·hīl* is a small dot placed over the second *alif* in place of the *hamzah* as in the following diagram:

ءَاْعْجَمِيٌّ وَعَرَبِيٌّ

Pronounce the second *hamzah* in 41:44 as a hybrid between *hamzah* and *alif*

Imālah

Imālah means to make one thing incline toward another. In *tajwīd* it refers to the special way that ا is pronounced in the word مَجْرَاهَا in 11:41 according to the transmission of Ḥafṣ from ʿĀṣim. In particular, we pronounce this ا as a hybrid between an *alif* and a *yā'*. The notation for *imālah* is a small dot placed under the ر as in the following diagram:

بِسۡمِ ٱللَّهِ مَجۡر۪اهَا

Pronounce the *alif* in 11:41 as a hybrid between an alif and a *yā'*

ن *al-Quṭnīyyah*

Whenever we find a *tanwīn* followed by a *hamzat al-waṣl* (ٱ), we must treat the *tanwīn* as a *nūn sākinah* (as we mentioned in the chapter on that subject) and then place a *kasrah* on it. See the following example and note what is happening behind the scenes.

نُوحٌ ٱبْنَهُ	←	نُوحُنْ ٱبْنَهُ	←	نُوحُنِ ٱبْنَهُ

Hamzat al-Waṣl

Hamzat al-waṣl (ٱ) poses a challenge for those who do not know Arabic morphology. Hopefully, you already know that ٱ is omitted altogether when a word beginning with it connects with the preceding word as in the following examples:

وَشَّمۡس	=	وَٱلشَّمۡس
وَجۡتَنِبُواْ	=	وَٱجۡتَنِبُواْ
وَلَّذِي	=	وَٱلَّذِي

The challenge comes when a sentence or phrase begins with a ٱ because its vowel is never written on it, as you can see in the following examples:

ٱَلْحَقُّ مِن رَّبِّكَ	=	ٱلْحَقُّ مِن رَّبِّكَ
ٱَلَّذِينَ يُؤْمِنُونَ بِٱلْغَيْبِ	=	ٱلَّذِينَ يُؤْمِنُونَ بِٱلْغَيْبِ
ٱِعْمَلُوا۟ مَا شِئْتُمْ	=	ٱعْمَلُوا۟ مَا شِئْتُمْ
ٱِهْدِنَا ٱلصِّرَٰطَ ٱلْمُسْتَقِيمَ	=	ٱهْدِنَا ٱلصِّرَٰطَ ٱلْمُسْتَقِيمَ
ٱُدْعُ إِلَىٰ سَبِيلِ رَبِّكَ	=	ٱدْعُ إِلَىٰ سَبِيلِ رَبِّكَ

Because the vowel is not written, it is important that you learn the rules for ٱ so that you can read it correctly at the beginning of such phrases.

You should use the following rules for deciding which *ḥarakah* to give to ٱ:

Rule 1: The ٱ in ٱل always takes a *fatḥah* as in the words ٱلشَّمْس and ٱلْقَمَر. You can extend this rule to words like ٱلَّتِي, ٱلَّذِي, ٱلَّذِينَ, and ٱللَّاتِي even though the ٱل at the beginning of these words is not considered the definite particle ٱل by most grammarians.

Rule 2: The only instance when ٱ takes a *ḍammah* is in imperative verbs and passive verbs where there is a *ḍammah* after the first *sukūn*. More simply stated, look for the following pattern:

ٱ + ـْ + ـُ

When you see this pattern, you will almost always do well to give the ٱ a *ḍammah*.[8] If you look at the following examples, you will

[8] I say "almost always" because there are, in fact, instances when it seems you have the pattern above, but you still have to give the ٱ a *kasrah*. Understanding the reason for this apparent inconsistency requires more knowledge of Arabic grammar than I can justify offering you at this juncture. Suffice it to say that the *ḍammah* that follows the *sukūn* in these instances did not originally belong after the *sukūn*. It belonged to a letter that has since been omitted and whose *ḍammah* has been transferred to its current location. In reality these words belong in Rule 3. The following table shows some examples, how to pronounce them, and provides a glimpse at the original state of the verbs before they were modified to their current state, respectively:

(ٱِقْضِيُوا۟)	ٱِقْضُوا۟	=	ٱقْضُوا۟
(ٱِبْنِيُوا۟)	ٱِبْنُوا۟	=	ٱبْنُوا۟
(ٱِمْشِيُوا۟)	ٱِمْشُوا۟	=	ٱمْشُوا۟
(ٱِئْتِيُونِي)	ٱِئْتُونِي	=	ٱئْتُونِي

understand what I am saying:

ٱُنْظُرْ	=	ٱنْظُرْ
ٱُخْرُجْ	=	ٱخْرُجْ
ٱُدْعُ	=	ٱدْعُ
ٱُدْخُلْ	=	ٱدْخُلْ
ٱُسْكُنْ	=	ٱسْكُنْ

Thankfully, the instances of this phenomenon are few in the Qur'ān, and if you abide by the conventions for stopping (*waqf*), you will rarely have to face this issue. The only instance you will likely face occurs in Qur'ān 46:4. There is an optional stopping point (*waqf*) before the word ٱئْتُونِي. You will do well to simply memorize this word and its correct pronunciation rather than to try and remember the grammar behind it.

__Note__: The word ٱئْتُونِي in the aforementioned verse offers another interesting twist. If you choose to stop before this word and start afresh on it, you will end up with two vocalized *hamzahs* at the beginning of this word: one is *hamzat al-waṣl* (ٱ); the other is *hamzat al-qaṭ'* (ء). In Arabic morphology, this is not allowed. In such instances, we must change the second *hamzah* into a ي. The end result will be to pronounce the word as ٱِيتُونِي. If you listen carefully to Khalīl al-Ḥuṣarī's or Muḥammad Ṣiddīq al-Minshāwī's recitation of this verse, you will notice that they observe this rule correctly.

اُضْطُرَّ	=	ٱضْطُرَّ
اُسْتُهْزِئَ	=	ٱسْتُهْزِئَ
اُسْتُضْعِفُوا۟	=	ٱسْتُضْعِفُوا۟

Rule 3: In all other instances of ٱ, it takes a *kasrah*. Therefore, if the ٱ is not part of ٱل and you have determined that rule 2 does not apply, you should give ٱ a *kasrah*. The following table lists a small sampling of the many instances of this rule:

اِهْدِنَا	=	ٱهْدِنَا
اِقْرَأْ	=	ٱقْرَأْ
اِعْمَلُوا۟	=	ٱعْمَلُوا۟
اِسْتَأْجِرْهُ	=	ٱسْتَأْجِرْهُ
اِنْتَصَرُوا۟	=	ٱنْتَصَرُوا۟
اِبْتِغَاءَ	=	ٱبْتِغَاءَ
اِسْتِغْفَارُ	=	ٱسْتِغْفَارُ

ٱِمْرَأَةُ ٱلْعَزِيزِ	=	ٱمْرَأَةُ ٱلْعَزِيزِ
ٱِبْنَتَ عِمْرَانَ	=	ٱبْنَتَ عِمْرَانَ
ٱِثْنَتَا عَشْرَةَ عَيْناً	=	ٱثْنَتَا عَشْرَةَ عَيْناً
ٱِسْمُهُ أَحْمَدُ	=	ٱسْمُهُ أَحْمَدُ

Key to Symbols in the *ʿUthmān Ṭahā* Convention

At the end of most copies of the Qurʾān written in the *ʿUthmān Ṭāhā* convention, there is a list and description of all the symbols and shorthands he has employed. I have collected these symbols and shorthands here along with a brief description of their meaning and some illustrative examples.

۠ Over a long vowel → Letter is non-essential; do not pronounce it	ءَامَنُواْ = ءَامَنُو لَأَاْذْبَحَنَّ = لَأَذْبَحَنَّ
0 Over an *alif* → Do not pronounce *alif* when connecting to next word	أَنَا۠ خَيْرٌ مِّنْهُ = أَنَ خَيْرٌ مِّنْهُ

ْ Over a letter → The letter is *sākin* and must be pronounced with *iẓhār*	مِنْ إِلَٰهٍ قَدْ سَمِعَ
Nothing over letter followed by *shaddah* → Complete *idghām*	وَلَمْ يَكُن لَّهُ عَبَدتُّمْ
Nothing over letter – not followed by *shaddah* → Either partial *idghām or ikhfā'*	وَإِن يَرَوْا مِن دُونِ وَمَا هُم بِمُؤْمِنِينَ

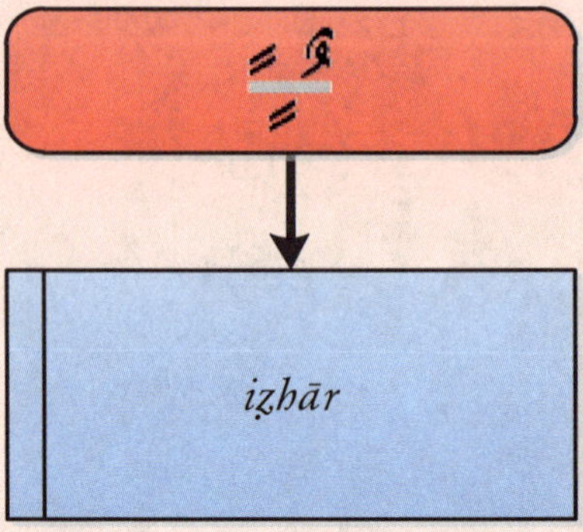

رِزْقًا حَسَنًا

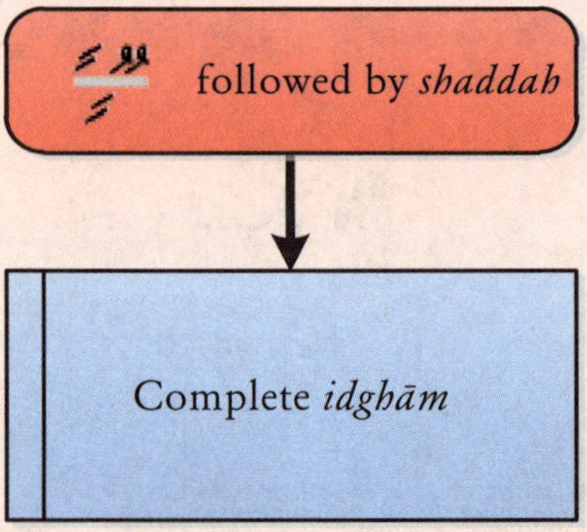

مُحَمَّدٌ رَّسُولُ اللَّهِ

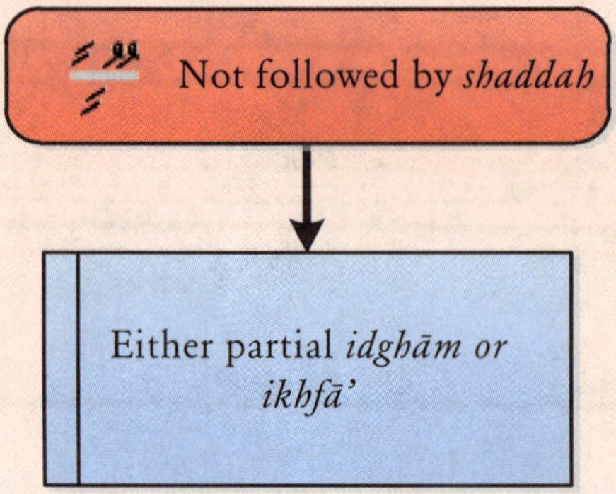

خَيْرًا يَرَهُ

عَزِيزٌ ذُو انتِقَامٍ

Small ۢ ↓ *iqlāb*	مِنۢ بَعۡدِ سَمِيعَۢا بَصِيرٗا
Small ا و ن ے ↓ *Letters omitted from the original ʻUthmānic copies. They must be pronounced.*	ذَٰلِكَ ٱلۡكِتَٰبُ دَاوُۥدُ يُحۡيِۦ نُـۨجِي
Small ٰ over a و or ي ↓ Pronounce the small ٰ in place of the و or ي	كَمِشۡكَوٰةٖ مُوسَىٰ

Small س over ص → س is preferred to ص	وَيَبۡصُۜطُ
Small س under ص → ص is preferred to س	ٱلۡمُصَۣيۡطِرُونَ
~ → Any *madd* longer than *al-madd al-ṭabīʿ ī*	ٱلسَّمَآءُ

● Below a letter ↓ Pronounce the *alif* as a hybrid between an *alif* and a *yā'*	بِسۡمِ ٱللَّهِ مَجۡر۪ىٰهَا
● Above an *alif* ↓ Pronounce *hamzah* as a hybrid between *hamzah* and *alif*	ءَا۬عۡجَمِيّٞ وَعَرَبِيّٞ
ص Above an *alif* ↓ *Hamzat al-waṣl* must be dropped when connecting to what precedes it.	بِسۡمِ ٱللَّهِ

(٦) → Marks number of previous verse	Unlike the English convention, in the Qur'ān you will find the verse number *after* the verse.
❋ → Marks the beginning of a quarter *ḥizb*	A *ḥizb* is a half of a *juz'* which is 1/30 of the Qur'ān
---- Over words → Marks words that make *sajdah* compulsory or recommended	See 3:15 and 96:19

 ↓ Marks end of verse where *sajdah* is compulsory or recommended	There are 15 *sajdah* verses in the Qur'ān: 11 make *sajdah mustaḥabb*. 4 make *sajdah wājib*. They are: 1) *al-Sajdah* 32:15 2) *Fuṣṣilat* 41:37 (note that the symbol is in the wrong place in most copies of the Qur'ān) 3) *al-Najm* 53:62 4) *al-'Alaq* 96:19
Small س above the end of a word ↓ Marks a *saktah*. Pause without taking a breath.	See 83:14

مـ ↓ الوقف لازم You must stop	See 6:36
ج ↓ الوقف جائز You may stop	See 18:13
صلى ↓ الوصل أولى It is better to continue	See 6:17

قلى الوقف أولى It is better to stop	See 18:22
∴ ∴ المعانقة If you stop at one, you must not stop at the other	See 2:2

Tajwīd according to Islamic Law

Until now we have covered all the major rules of *tajwīd*. Pronouncing the Qur'ān according to these rules certainly makes our recitation attractive and lends uniformity to the recitation of various people. However, we have yet to view these rules from a legal perspective to see which among them we are obligated to follow and which we can legally forgo. I will now give you an overview of the legal requirements for practicing *tajwīd* in Qur'ānic recitation.[9] Specifically, we shall delve into the rulings for using *tajwīd* when reciting the Qur'ān in the obligatory prayers. Aside from the obligatory prayers, reciting the Qur'ān is not obligatory—though it is highly recommended—so whether one uses *tajwīd* or not is a moot point.

[9] All legal rulings referred to here are based on the rulings of Sayyid 'Ali al-Sīstānī in *Minhāj al-Ṣāliḥīn*.

Recitation of *sūrat al-fātiḥah* and another complete *sūrah* is an obligatory part of the prayer. It is critical that we know how much of *tajwīd* we must abide by to qualify our recitation and thereby our prayers.

The basic formulation of our duty is that we must read with good Arabic pronunciation. More explicitly, we are obligated to do the following:

1. Pronounce all the letters from their correct points of articulation so that they sound Arabic. Of course, if this is not possible, then we must simply do the best we can.[10]
2. Pronounce all *ḥarakah*s and *sukūn*s as they are written.[11]
3. Omit *hamzat al-waṣl* when connecting it to what precedes it.[12]
4. Pronounce *hamzat al-qaṭʿ* in all circumstances.[13]
5. Do *idghām* of the definite particle *lām* into the sun letters.[14]
6. Do not do *idghām* of the definite particle *lām* into the moon letters.[15]

---

[10] Al-Sīstānī, ʿAlī. *Minhāj al-Ṣāliḥīn*. vol. 1, p.207, issue #606.

[11] *ibid.*

[12] *ibid.* issue #607

[13] *ibid.* issue #607

[14] *ibid.* p. 208, issue #611

7. Pronounce the *madd* only where it is *lāzim muthaqqal*, that too, only to the extent that the *shaddah* is made clear.[16]

If you now realize that you have not been abiding by some of these obligatory rules in the recitation during your prayers, and all the while, you believed that you were reciting correctly, then your past prayers are correct. Simply make the correction in your prayers from now on.[17]

None of the other rules of *tajwīd* are obligatory. Sayyid al-Sīstāni has singled out the following *tajwīd* rules as being recommended:

1. *idghām* of *nūn sākinah* into the letters of يرملون[18]
2. *idghām* in the general sense[19]
3. *nūn al-quṭnīyyah*[20]
4. the rules for *waqf*[21]

---

[15] *ibid.* issue #611

[16] *ibid.* issue #609

[17] *ibid.* p. 209, issue #615

[18] *ibid.* p. 208, issue #610

[19] *ibid.* issue #612

[20] *ibid.* p. 209, issue #614

[21] *ibid.* p. 207, issue #608

Afterword

Tajwīd is meant to be a practical science, not a theoretical one. It is next to useless to know the rules if we are not willing to implement them and improve our recitation. While it is true that not all the rules of *tajwīd* are obligatory, abiding by all of them holds some benefit. Something that is aesthetically appealing is more likely to move us emotionally and perhaps spiritually. It is also more likely to attract others to want to know the meaning of what is being recited.

In any case, you can only hope to be able to implement these rules if you practice them. This book is meant only to introduce you to the rules and explain to you how to implement them. The actual implementation and the proficiency of implementation depend solely on you. I suggest that you read along with the famous reciter Khalīl al-Ḥuṣarī, since he is arguably the most precise of all reciters in implementing the rules of *tajwīd*.

May God make us all proficient in reading the Qur'ān.

May he make our recitation a source of blessing and reward for us.

May our recitation be the first step toward comprehension, contemplation, and righteous action.

And may God shower the Prophet Muḥammad and his family with his mercy.

Sources

Al-Sīstānī, ʿAlī. *Minhāj al-Ṣāliḥīn*. Mashhad, Iran: Sunbulah, 2004

Surty, Muhammad Ibrahim H.I. *A Course in the Science of Reciting the Qur'ān*. Leicester, UK: The Islamic Foundation, 1992

Khan, Abdul-Majid. *Tajwīd: The Art of Recitation of the Holy Qur'an*. Karachi: Urdu Academy Sind, 1992

Ḥabībī, ʿAlī and Muḥammad Razā Shahīdī. *Ravānkhānī wa tajwīd-e qur'an-e karīm*. Qum: Rūḥānī, 2001

Al-Ḥuṣarī, Maḥmūd Khalīl. *Aḥkām qirā'at al-qur'ān al-karīm*. 4th ed. *Al-Maktabah al-Makkiyyah* and *Dār al-Bashā'ir*, 1999